LET KIDS BE KIDS

Raising Happy, Healthy, and Safe Children

DR SUSIE O'NEILL

COPYRIGHT

Published by:
SeeMore's Publishing House,
Noosa Heads, Queensland, Australia.

ISBN: 978-0-6451665-3-8

PUBLICATION INFORMATION

The information and ideas provided in this book are based on the author's personal experiences of working with thousands of children in the health and education sectors as well as the findings from a 10-year doctoral study "Developing Safety Risk Intelligence in Children".

A bird sitting on a tree is never afraid of the branch breaking because her trust is not on the branch but on her own wings. Always believe in yourself.

Unknown

FOR MY GRANDCHILDREN

To Bailey, Chase, Nellie, Lewi, Frankie, Bowie, Alfie and Bella who are happy, healthy, and safe and have a good balance of "free-range". Love you heaps. x

FOR MY OTHER KIDS

This book is inspired by all the children who found their way into the KIDS Foundation life. They are the most inspirational and courageous little people who have suffered trauma, harm, and injury that most of us could not imagine.

LET KIDS BE KIDS

Raising Happy, Healthy, and Safe Children

Dr Susie O'Neill

FOREWORD BY DR RICHARD HARRIS

Dr Susie O'Neill is a warrior, fighting for the rights of children to live a safe and happy life. Hence it is a privilege to have been asked to pen a few words to introduce this guide for *LET KIDS BE KIDS: Raising Happy, Healthy, and Safe Children.*

Planet Earth is a dangerous place, yet it has never been so safe for most of us. We no longer need to forage for food, or to hunt and gather. Shelter is a basic human right as is the right to feel safe in one's own home. Humans control everything around them, living in temperature-controlled environments with food from the shop safely stored in the refrigerator. We are more educated than ever before, living longer and physically more comfortable than we have ever been. Modern medicine, vaccinations, antibiotics, clean drinking water, and preventative health measures will result in a longevity never before experienced. Of course, much of what I say is only true for Australia, while many countries are not so fortunate. And Indigenous Australians still suffer a massive gap in all these areas.

However, given that most of us are seeing the benefits of living in the "lucky country", why are we more worried about our kids than ever? Why is there a perceived explosion of mental health issues in our youth?

While life has changed for the better for most Australians over recent decades, there have been some very obvious changes in society. In my view, one large issue is that despite the advent of the smartphone and social media, where degrees of separation mean you seem to know almost everyone, we have never felt so disconnected from our community. At the risk of sounding like the 50-something man I am, "when I was a lad," we would know every kid in the street and roam the neighbourhood with our tribe. We knew all the parents, and any misdemeanours would rapidly be reported to our parents. While the old-fashioned model of a stay-at-home mum and a hard-working dad does not suit contemporary society, it did mean we all sat at the table at night for dinner and we talked. And family holidays were never an overseas trip to Bali. They involved renting a beach house or staying at a mate's shack on the river. We did outdoor stuff as a family. Smartphones and the internet had not even been imagined, so we really engaged with each other. It was loud; it was boisterous; but it was family.

Back in the day, if there was trouble at school, it stayed at school, and at least you had the night off from it. Bullying didn't follow you home on your phone. Online predators didn't exist. Bad people were out there, of course, more so than today according to the statistics. In fact, the rate of kidnapping in Australia has fallen dramatically from 2008, which coincides with the release of the first iPhone. I'm not linking these events, but it is interesting that our paranoia about predators has increased up at the same time as the rate has actually fallen.

Unfortunately, injury does remain the leading cause of death in children aged one to16 years in Australia, and hospitalisation rates have not decreased for over the past 10 years. And for every child who dies, many more are injured. Although the hard numbers of fatalities are very gradually improving, transport accidents, drownings, and assaults remain the leading causes.

What am I getting at with all this information? I'll summarise by saying that, overall, kids are safer than they have ever been, but there remains a large group of children for whom accident prevention strategies are very important. And, sadly, large numbers of children for whom post-injury and burns support services will always be required. The KIDS Foundation is doing an admirable job in both these spaces.

But there is a less obvious problem, which I sense is yet to fully unveil itself in the physical and mental wellbeing of the young people of Australia. While the physical safety of our kids slowly improves, another insidious problem might be arising. The lack of independence, the loss of connection with your "tribe", the decrease in physical robustness and mental toughness that comes with being outside and testing yourself against the environment; all these qualities are being eroded due to the increase in indoor screen time and the well intentioned "cotton wool" or "helicopter" parenting that is born out of fear for the wellbeing of our kids. If kids aren't allowed to climb trees, kick the footy, or ride their bikes around the neighbourhood with their mates after school, we might just breed a generation of obese, vitamin D deficient introverts who don't even speak to their parents at mealtimes because the whole family is staring at their phones.

It's a difficult balance to strike. I am a parent. I was nervous about my kids riding to school because the roads are far busier than they used to be. But I tried my best to bite my tongue when my boys announced that they were heading out to skateboard down the nearest hill or take their BMX bikes to the skate park. "Be home for tea at 6." That's what Mum used to say to me, and I think that should be the message for the current generation of kids. There will be stitches; there will be arms in casts; there will be dental bills. And very occasionally tragedy will strike. But the majority of children will be better adults as a result of finding a little independence. And when things don't go well, thank goodness Susie O'Neill and the KIDS foundation will be there to help.

Dr Richard Harris & Dr Susie O'Neill

THINGS THAT MATTER

✓ The year before school
✓ Family values
✓ Healthy practises
✓ Mindset
✓ Handling things (2 ways/2 outcomes)
✓ What is real and what is a myth
✓ Experiences you give them
✓ Decisions you make

OUR PASSION

Dr Susie O'Neill and Dr Richard Harris share a passion in wanting children to have a hands-on approach to learning, exploring their environment, and experiencing what the great outdoors offers in order to adapt and learn in a way that just lets kids be kids.

There is no simple answer for parents to ensure their child's future happiness, health, and safety. You are sure to have experienced others wanting to give their opinions. Thank them for it, and take in what resonates with your parenting values. Their advice might not be right for you or your child; just trust your own judgement. In saying that, take from this book the things you are comfortable with and would like to implement. And one other simple message is "if they are capable of doing it, don't do it for them."

DR SUSIE O'NEILL

Susie has a Doctor of Philosophy of Education and is a qualified preschool and primary teacher who specialises in working with children at risk. Her interest in empowering children to protect themselves began in 1988 when she was studying teaching at the Ballarat College of Advanced Education and working alongside the Children's Protection Society. Susie has dedicated her studies and career to children at risk, where her focus has been on educating them to prevent and recover from trauma, harm and injuries.

Susie has written 13 children's books, many of which have been focused around a character she created named SeeMore Safety. She has had three journal papers published, presented numerous peer-reviewed national and international conference papers and won awards for her contribution to the field of childhood injury prevention.

My daughter, Emma, who is extremely health focused, had paid to go to a health retreat in Bali. The retreat was focused on healthy eating and habits. Unexpectedly, she fell pregnant and suffered from severe morning sickness, so she suggested I take her place. "What could I possibly learn from something like this? I'm already healthy, so I thought." This was an eye-opener. At nearly 60, I had no idea what really healthy meant — the importance of things I took for granted. Simple things like breathing, drinking water, eating wholefoods, getting out in the sunshine, exercising, having a passion, and sharing good relationships. All things that impact on a healthy life. I had always prided myself on being what I thought of as a really health-conscious mum. This was a wake-up call, and if I had my time again, I would do things very differently. Combined with what I had learnt from that experience at the retreat and 42 years of trying to be the best mum, the greatest nanny, the perfect friend, and the first-class teacher, which by the way, I'm none of these. But I do the best I can.

What is shared in this book may not be for everyone. That's okay, but if it helps some in the smallest of ways to making their child's life happier, healthier, and safer, then it has been all worthwhile.

In 1979, at the age of 19, I began working alongside the Children's Protection Society while studying teaching at the Ballarat College of Advanced Education. I remember receiving this letter that read: "Her interest and enthusiasm is unusual in one so young, and indicates a genuine interest in the 'at risk' child." This was probably the reason I chose the path I did and dedicated my life to empowering at-risk children.

My professional career in preschool and primary school teaching began in 1981 when I got my first job. In the mornings, I was a kindergarten teacher at a day care centre, and in the afternoons, I was a specialist art and physical education teacher at a private primary school. The day care position turned out to be the most perfect job for me because my husband, Brett, and I were eager to start a family, and it meant that in working in a day care centre, I would be able to take our children with me. For the next nine and a half years I stayed in that position and had four beautiful children during that time — Matt in 1982, Emma in 1984, Ben in 1988, and Kate in 1990.

It was quite challenging to turn up to work on my first day at the centre to find the little people I was about to teach had an extremely wide range of varying abilities. Most of the children had higher than average IQs. Several children were classified as "gifted" and belonged to the Association for Gifted and Talented Children. This encouraged me to design a curriculum that challenged them all. On Mondays and Thursdays, we had classroom activities, and Tuesdays we spent time at the Ballarat Library. On Wednesdays, we visited the Queen Elizabeth Geriatric Centre (QEGC), where the children participated in an intergenerational program created to connect the elderly residents and the children called "Adopt a Grandparent". On Fridays, we arranged swimming lessons at a local pool. By the end of the year the children left kinder, they all had strong water survival capabilities and could confidently swim 25 metres.

This experience led me to establishing a foundation. There was a 12-year-old boy who was sleeping in a ward with three gentlemen in their 90s. I felt this wasn't a healthy environment for a young person to be in. At the time, rehabilitation centres that purposely catered for children didn't exist. It disturbed me to think that this was the case. I went home and discussed the situation with Brett, who is a tradie. He agreed to help me create a child-friendly space, raise funds, and get his tradie mates to also help. This encouraged me in 1993 to establish a foundation — KIDS (Kids In Dangerous Situations) to try to get what we needed donated.

Billie and Philip at the aged care centre

We were designated an old dining room within the grounds of the aged-care facility to renovate. Right before the renovation was to commence, the government provided a refurbishment grant, which meant the whole facility was going to be upgraded. Therefore, the money we had raised could be directed towards equipment, activities, and facilities for the children. The accommodation section of the new development opened in the mid '90s. The first young person to stay in the accommodation was a survivor with horrific burn injuries. When the day came for him to return home, there were no support networks to assist with his recovery outside the comfort zone of the hospital. That was when the KIDS established the Burn Survivors' Network, which was incorporated into the Injury Recovery program. The term "survivor" is important and reflects the philosophy of what we practise at the KIDS Foundation, which empowers the healing process. In 2000, we stood at the opening proudly representing the Foundation after being integral in the process of making it happen. It was named "Pete's Place", built on the grounds of the QEGC. Pete's Place was one of the first children's rehabilitation centres in Australia. Today, it is used by more than 600 children each year for day therapies as well as for the occasional stay.

KIDS Foundation

The KIDS Foundation is a special place to work. Every day the team devote its time and resources to help survivors rebuild their lives as well as empowering and educating children and their families on ways to prevent the emotional and physical injuries and trauma associated with events that put children in dangerous situations. That is where KIDS gets its acronym from – "Kids In Dangerous Situations."

The children supported in our recovery programs have survived the most unimaginable horrific injuries and trauma caused by burns, accidents, dog attacks, crime, neglect, abuse, and environmental events. They are inspirational and courageous and remind us why we do what we do. Some of them you will get to meet in this book.

Susie with Brittney, Dalton and David at Camp Phoenix.

I strongly believe in the voice of the child, and the KIDS Foundation's work demonstrates the important role children play in their survival and safety learning. For some crazy reason in 2006, I accepted the offer to take on a doctoral study at Monash. Ten years on, I obtained my "Doctor of Philosophy in Education".

In my studies, I created the term "safety risk intelligence" to capture a child's ability to act with understanding when making choices that could potentially cause an injury. When children are given the right learning opportunities and experiences, I believe they can build safety risk intelligence that equips them with the capabilities they need to become competent risk-takers and manage everyday life and activities. Safety is all about making good choices. What my studies taught me was that being safe requires both a physical and emotional secure connection. It involves a holistic approach to establishing a strong understanding and awareness of self and what a child as an individual is capable of. There is an emotional attachment that requires you to feel secure both inside and out.

I believe we need to consider more broadly a child's wellbeing and think about their health and happiness so that it is not compromised in the context of their safety.

At the end of the day, we just need to let kids be kids.

Throw away the bubble wrap and just let kids be kids

If you find a way to do the things that seem impossible, anything is possible

Children with SeeMore and the storybook series.

FOREWORD
BY MICHAEL ADAMEDES

There is a saying. "It doesn't matter how much my mother loves me, I would never give her the scalpel to operate on my brain". It means that love and good intentions are not enough; knowledge and skills are also important.

Also, I wouldn't be happy to have a surgeon operate on my brain if he didn't like me. We need both love and knowledge.

After more than 40 years of clinical experience, the difficulties that I see most people face are often from unresolved childhood experiences. Their parents were loving and well meaning but lacked the skills or carried trauma from their own childhood.

The problem most people face is not from a lack of love or good intention while growing up; it's usually because the adults caring for them just didn't understand their needs. Often because those adults themselves didn't have their own needs met.

The first seven years of life are the most important time in a person's entire life. It's the time when the patterns of behaviour are imprinted into the personality. It's also the time when the child is most sensitive and most vulnerable.

Educating parents and caregivers to the needs of children is one of the most important things we can do for the future wellbeing of everyone in society.

The tremendous value contained in this book is that it explains practical common-sense methods for parents and carers to support children, while also providing a better understanding of the psychology that motivates a child's behaviour.

Michael Adamedes
michaeladamedes.com

FOREWORD BY PROF MARILYN FLEER
Australian Research Council Laureate Fellow

It is so exciting to see a quality publication that speaks directly to the lives of families with such an important message about keeping children safe. *LET KIDS BE KIDS: Raising Happy, Healthy, and Safe Children* is more than a how-to manual; it is a story about the everyday lives of children growing up safely with their families and in their local community.

Statistics can give a picture of how safe children are in a particular country or community, but figures do not tell us what that looks like for a family. Dr Susie O'Neill shares with us what it means to keep children safe in the water, through the quality of the air they breathe; through what they eat; how they can exercise; when in the sun; and much more. The breadth of what is covered in this publication is astounding. Every part of a child's wellbeing is considered, alongside important messages about connecting with how a child thinks about their own safety.

What is so special about this book is that it recognises that children are curious and amazing human beings, while also reminding us that they have not experienced the world for as long as we have. This means that they will have a different way of looking at the world and interpreting what they see.

A belief that children are capable of learning how to be safe, alongside the passion of the author for keeping them safe, jumps off every page of this book. This is a book that children and adults can read and enjoy together as they talk and enact staying safe and being healthy.

DID YOU KNOW?

Did you know that in Australia about 5000 children will present to a hospital emergency department each day because of injury? This is more than twice the number of hospital admissions for illness and disease combined, every year. However, injury just doesn't receive the same attention that curing disease and illness does. So much energy is poured into reactive measures to deal with attempts to bring down the alarming injury statistics. We are flooded with rules, regulations, and enforcements to deal with childhood injury problems, but rarely do these consider what children can bring to the solution.

The bubble-wrap and cotton-wool attitude just doesn't work. There is plenty of research around that tells us so. That doesn't negate the fact that childhood injury is a bigger problem than most of us realise.

In Australia about 5000 children will go to a hospital emergency department each day because of injury.

CONTENTS

NOTES

Making decisions about risk and safety is about whether your child is facing real or perceived danger and then taking a common-sense approach. I have no memories of running, doing forward rolls, climbing trees, going to playgrounds, swinging on monkey bars, and playing in sandpits as being "dangerous". They were fun activities that were full of adventure, and, yes, occasionally someone would get hurt. One of the greatest challenges as a parent is to find that balance, to way up the odds of the benefits versus the dangers, and then ask how real is it. For example, the common myths about "stranger danger". It is a fact that most children who have been abused received the abuse from someone known to them who they would usually trust, not by a stranger; and, most child abductions are committed by family members. Experts warn that the old "stranger danger" message can fail to protect them. Keeping children healthy and safe is everybody's business. It is the people who are in your child's life who need to create places where your child will feel safe; places where they will play, learn, grow, and feel confident — their safety zones. Think about the way you choose to raise your child and the counterproductive outcomes of overprotectiveness. The learning experiences you bring into your child's life are better than "bubble-wrap" solutions. Be the parent who gives their child the freedom to grow and provides them with safety learning so that they know how to be a "free-safe kid".

"Free to grow and safety to know"
— Dr Susie O'Neill

FREE-SAFE KIDS

A sign on the gate read: "Slow Down! Free-range Children".

I'm not sure whether it was the yummy freshly home-baked scones, jam, and farm cream or the children that enchanted my mind that day. This is the most vivid memory I have of the Coast to Coast track, walking into Ravenseat, one of the remote farms along the Yorkshire Dales. I had to read the sign over and over: "Slow Down! Free-range Children", and again "Slow Down! Free-range Children", not chickens, as I originally thought, actually children.

I was soon greeted by the famous model, shepherdess, and mother of six, with one on the way, and who in fact only had a day to go. Her children were swinging on the fences and hanging out of the trees. They had free run of the farm along with dogs, ponies, horses, and over 1000 sheep. The children were obviously being raised in the spirit of encouragement to function independently. There was plenty of sibling support appropriate to their stage of development and with a realistic perception of personal risk. There were no waivers to sign on this farm. The children were climbing trees, walking along the stone-wall fences, or wading in the creek; they were exploring their world.

I believe that children need a certain amount of this type of freedom, a bit of "free-range". Empowering children's independence, fostering their self-awareness, nurturing their sense of adventure, and encouraging them to learn through making mistakes and through managed risks is what is important.

The first three things you must do to raise a free-safe kid is to:

1. Throw away the bubble-wrap attitude and just let your kid be a kid.
2. Let your child know that their opinions matter; that you are listening; and that you value all the things that they bring to their own learning.
3. Get out and explore the real world with them to help them find their safe world.

HAPPY. HEALTHY. SAFE.

Ask yourself: What are the three things that you wish most for your child?

I guess you will have at least one or all three of these:

Happy. Healthy. Safe.

This book provides some ways for you to help your child find the self-awareness that will guide them to have a happy, healthy, and safe life and to help you raise that "free-safe kid".

SELF-AWARE BEHAVIOUR

How often do we hear "they are too young to know" or "they wouldn't understand". Actually, in many ways they are not too young to know, and in most cases they do understand, further more; they can play an important role in creating a solution to the problem. It's called "self-aware behaviour". There is nothing more rewarding than working with children and taking the time to listen to their ways of thinking. They have such simplistic and uncomplicated ways of seeing things. Kids are great teachers. We can learn so much from them, and they also have a valuable role to play in their own learning. With the right supportive attitude, we can build a generation of "free-safe kids" that are "safety risk intelligent" without the "bubble-wrap" solutions. The answer to preventing injuries is "safety", which is not something new, and most of the time it's just about making good choices. My view is that safety is a wholesome thing that needs a holistic approach. What I mean by this is that to be safe, you need to be secure inside and out, taking into consideration a child's physical and emotional safety.

Too often the safety solutions just deal with the outside – for example a bike helmet. These are all great at preventing injuries when they are used properly, or if used at all. In a way, more often than not, they can give us a false sense of security because we rely on these things. For example, at our house in the front yard, we have a pool that has all the required fencing, and in the backyard, we have a river that has no regulations. When the children are out the back, we do not lose eye contact for a second. We are always checking with each other making sure there is someone there for them. However, when the children go to the front yard, we perceive that it is safe, and if they happen to wander out, we tend to think it's okay — we have a pool fence, I'll check them in a minute. But, what happens if the latch on the gate fails or someone leaves it open? It can take as little as 30 seconds for a child to drown, and they usually do it quietly. If the drowning doesn't take the child's life, equally devasting is a near-drowning that can affect the function of a child's brain.

The day Hakavai fell into the pool

It was a glorious day in Hawaii. I'd spoken at a conference that day before, so Michael, Hakavai, and I were sitting by the pool for a little downtime before the trip home.

Hakavai was having the BEST time. His squeals of delight every time Michael threw him into the air reverberated around the amphitheatre the pool made.

It was one of those rare, golden, sunshine-y moments as a parent. A kind of smug but grateful moment.

I exchanged sweet smiles with the other pool-goers as they exclaimed, "What a gorgeous baby!" and lounged in the sun, basking in the knowledge that Michael was a great dad, our son was perfect, and that I, too, was an excellent wife and mother.

Michael and Hak got out of the pool and sat down beside me. But, now being a crawling and inquisitive kid, Hakavai kept creeping right up to the edge of the pool as if to go in. Every time he'd approach, Michael would pick him up and walk him back over to me on the grass. And then he'd crawl right back to the edge of the pool.

"Watch him, darling!" I instructed in strict tones.

"Yes, I am." I detected a subtle hint of irritation emanating from Michael.

"He might fall in."

"Nah, he'll be sweet."

And right at that moment, Hakavai fell in. It literally took half a second. There was a collective gasp from the tourists around the pool. Before my brain had even registered what was going on, Michael had plunged in. Action Man through and through!

He walked out of the pool, and popped Hak, safe and sound, back on firm ground.

Hak started laughing. And then crawled straight back to the edge of the pool. He's nothing if not committed to the cause!

That's the thing about kids, right? They're not deterred by setbacks.

If they want to do something, whether that's trying to stand or give their parents a heart attack trying to fling themselves into a pool, they don't let failure, or an imperfect attempt, stop them from trying again.

TURIA PITT

WHAT WOULD YOU DO?

In a situation similar to Hakavai's, where your child is crawling close to the edge of a pool, what would you do?

a. React by pulling them back with a negative remark like NO!
b. Take their hand and explain that if they get too close they could fall in.
c. Let them experience falling in where the risk of harm is low.
d. Don't take them to a pool again.
e. Put a floatation device on them when they are around pools.

NOTES

Think about your responses:

Outcomes to consider

a) Pulling them back with a negative remark like NO! This may teach them that water is "bad" and the experience would become negative.

b) Taking their hand and explaining that if they get too close they could fall in. It is always important to take the time to explain it as you never know when that "light-bulb moment" kicks in.

c) Let them experience falling in where the risk of harm is low. If you are okay with this and confident in the water, then by letting them experience falling in shows them that this is what happens when they fall in. Their emotional experience will either be, "This is fun! I want to go again because a person I trust is there to get me," as was the case for Hakavai. Or they may cry and decide not to do it again. Their response will be based on their personality, inherited traits, and experiences that you have given them.

d) Don't take them to a pool again. If you don't, how will they know and learn?

e) Put a floatation device on them when they are around pools. This is not a bad idea, but like the pool fences, it can give them a false sense of security. You will still need to be there with a watchful eye.

These responses are just some ways of thinking, and yours may be a little different, and that's okay as long as the risk is limited and you are helping your child experience water in a way that gives them a foundation to be safe around it. If you are not confident around water, it is important to have someone that is to ensure the child feels secure and to enable them to progress. The goal is that by the time they reach the "light-bulb" moment, they understand their capabilities around water.

WATER AWARENESS

At this stage of his development, Hakavai would most probably not understand the concept of water potentially being unsafe and actually probably never will. The same as for his parents, water will most probably become his happy place. They will provide him with lots of experiences in water, teach him to swim, and keep that watchful eye on him until their confidence has grown enough to allow him to be independent in the water. This is the time when your child will have the "light-bulb" moment, an understanding of what they are capable of doing in the water in their "safe zone". So, until your child has that light-bulb moment (something talked about in the next section), you need to be there for them regardless of those external measures that are in place.

Tips for raising super water-safe kids

1. Watch them and be present the whole time.

2. Give them lots of different water experiences.

3. Abide by the regulations and the rules such as swimming between the yellow and red flags at the beach. This shows you that it is the safest place to swim or play in the water, and as well as your eyes, there are other sets of eyes watching the area where you are with your child.

4. Teach them to swim or take them to swimming lessons. There are programs for children that start as young as six months old and even younger. Here they are taught to fall in and recover.

5. Instruct them to put on approved safety flotation devices in and around boats and other waterways.

6. Select appropriate safe swimming places. Dams and water canals are not safe places for swimming.

7. Teach them to always swim with a responsible person and never swim alone.

So many things we do are just automatic for us, and we forget that children need to be taught to do things like cross the road.

Here are some ideas when teaching road safety to children:

One
Find the safest place to cross.

Two
Each time you come to cross the road, take their hand and remember to stop every single time and say to them, "Let's cross here safely."

Three
Tell them to open their ears and listen for traffic.

Four
Teach them the "STOP SEE SAFE" saying: STOP to SEE if it is SAFE to GO.
See by looking to the left, looking to the right and the left again. If it is safe to go, say to them,
"Any cars?" Okay,
"Now it's safe to go!"

Five
Then walk straight across without running.

Six
If it is at a crossing, get them to look at the signal, point out the person walking, and explain the red means it is not safe to go, so they stop and wait. The green person tells them when they can cross. But it is still important to get them to look left, look right, then left again.
Say, "Any cars?" Okay,
"Now it's safe to go!"

EMPOWERING INDEPENDENCE

As your child becomes more confident, they will probably rebel against having their hand held. When that happens, let your child have some control by reversing the role-playing. Ask them to take your hand and help you cross the road. Once they have mastered this, and by the time they can cross by themselves, you will have empowered their independence, and safe habits will have been embedded.

One

Do you allow them to make appropriate choices for their stage of development. For example:

- Choosing their own clothes
- Letting them select their own food
- Engaging them in appropriate decision-making
- Letting them choose activities they may like to do
- Allowing them free playtime

Two

Do you allow them to do stage-appropriate things like:

- Dress themselves
- Brush their own teeth
- Get a glass of water
- Give them appropriate tasks

Three

Do you let your child choose their friends?
Here are some things to consider.

- Do you let them choose who they play with at kindergarten/preschool?

- Do you allow them to engage with other children besides your friend's children?

- Do you make judgements about other children in front of your child?

- Do you give them uninterrupted free play time to share with their friends?

- Do you teach them how to choose friends wisely?

Four

Do you allow your child to experience failure? Some things to ask yourself:

- Do you rescue them when they are experiencing a problem?

- Do you let them avoid situations where they can potentially fail?

- If they don't get invited to a party, do you contact the parents of the other child?

- Do you stop your child from taking risks?

- Do you let them tie their own shoelaces?

MAKING CHOICES

Let them make choices that are not influenced by your preferences and accept them. Steering their decisions sends a message that there is a wrong and right way, and their opinions are not valued. The way you frame a simple question matters: "What would you like to wear?" compared to "Would you like to wear this top?" The first question gives the child complete autonomy in making a choice; the framing of the second question robs your child of the opportunity to make a decision without the pressure of "wearing a top because you like it." No harm will come because of what your child decides to wear; however, when a child makes a choice that could result in an injury, you need to guide them in a way that helps them to understand that it wasn't a good choice and explain why. For example, if your child chooses to wear thongs when riding a bike, you could explain that thongs aren't a good choice because you could stub your toe on the path as the pedal goes around.

It is a progressive thing. Some kids will have just a few goes and will be off on their own; others may take much longer and may need more encouragement and praise. You will have helped your child through what we consider a shared learning activity, where you support them to develop their capabilities. The social aspect is so important because your child is working with you to help develop these new skills. The gaining of confidence is twofold, such as in the next scenario: your child gains the confidence to cross the monkey bars, and you gain the confidence to let them do it on their own. This is an example of helping them to discover that "light-bulb" moment.

A BIG-KID THING

If your child is wanting to copy and do a "big-kid" thing, an activity that you might consider unsafe, rather than dismiss the activity, look for ways to build their skills. Preventing your child from doing the things that you think are not safe, just like the swimming scenario, means that if you don't teach them, how will they know?

Let's use the monkey bars as a setting. Steps you can take:

1. Guide and lead the action while supporting them from one side to the other.

2. Let them initiate the action, but still be there to support them.

3. Let them attempt to do it unaided, but be there to catch them if they fall.

4. Once they have gained enough confidence and strength in their ability to cross, let them have a go.

THE LIGHT-BULB MOMENT

Children are little sponges who soak up so much right from when they enter this world, and the learning never stops. I went in search of the time when kids could really start deciding the type of person they wanted to become. There was a desire of wanting to know that stage when they would turn on that "light-bulb" and begin to take ownership of their own learning and emotions, shape their personality, and develop their own ways of thinking and doing, with UNDERSTANDING.

Not to take away from the great Greek philosopher, Aristotle, who once said, *"Give me a child until he is seven and I will show you the man."* Consider *"A child the year before they go to school is the 'self-aware' adult to be."*

I could go on about the academic and scientific reasons why "the year before your child goes to school," but it will bore some. However, if you are that way inclined, jump to the back of the book to the "WANT TO KNOW MORE" section where it goes a little deeper into the theories. You will notice that throughout the book there is not too much talk about age as a stage of readiness for safety learning. Age is often used as a guide, but every child is an individual with different capabilities based on all the things you, your parents, and your ancestors have given them and the environments that go with them. The mix of genes and situations has given your child their personality.

PERSONALITY

If you are a parent of more than one child, how many times do you say to yourself, "I have three (or however many children), who have been raised the same, but they are so different; they have very different personalities."

Here is an activity you can do with yourself:

One
Write down the qualities/personalities of your children: Child 1, 2 and 3.

Two
Note the similarities and differences.

Three
What are the clear things about each of your children that relate to you and the other biological parent?

You may find that one child has a different mix or a greater number of traits from one parent than the other.

Did you know that about 90 percent of your child's personality is made up of all the conscious and unconscious things that they have inherited from you, your parents, grandparents, and ancestors? They include learned positive and powerful qualities, but also negativity and self-limiting beliefs. The reason their personalities are different to those of their sisters or brothers is because they have inherited a different mix of inherited and learned traits.

The good news is that when you have things about yourself you don't like, you have the ability to change them. This can only really happen once you have accepted responsibility for certain things and events in your life. Throw away the blame game and deal with them. Your child can also change the things about themselves that they don't like that have been influenced by you, once they have also accepted responsibility for events in their lives. There are three adaptable things that determine the quality of our lives: genetics, environment, and the ability to be in touch with their emotional and mental self. You can't change the past, but you can learn from it to give you the power to determine your best future.

TURIA

This brings to mind a person previously mentioned, whom some of you may have met or seen in the media, who, despite all the odds, pushed through to achieve the greatest physical and mental transformation in order to overcome challenges and accomplish her greatest goals. Her name is Turia Pitt, who in 2011 had her life changed in a split moment by a fire. If through the lessons she has learnt and shares through her books and online programs, we could apply to our own and children's lives, we would build a generation of resilient, capable, and super safe self-achievers. She says she is grateful for all the things that the fire has taught her, and her father's parenting skills, which played a part in building the resilience that is instilled in her. However, she talks about practising gratitude as the single most life-changing part of her life — being thankful and showing appreciation for all the good and bad times in her life.

SELF

NOTES

Your child has endless potential that can be developed. There are two things you can do to influence their personality. The first is to guide them to release their self-limiting beliefs. What is meant by self-limiting is that sometimes we talk ourselves into believing that we are not capable of doing what we are trying to achieve. The second is to instil a positive mindset.

You may well ask, *"What does this have to do with injury prevention?"* By the time you have finished reading this book, you will know why it matters that what you think, feel, and believe inside will reflect how you respond to life on the outside and the choices you make.

How you see and perceive things will directly affect how your child views the world. Are you the glass half-full or the glass half-empty sort of person?

HALF EMPTY?
HALF FULL?

NEGATIVE SELF-TALK

You can choose to be your own worst enemy or greatest fan, it's all up to you. It's about the way you think of and talk about yourself.

Adamedes' triad of primary self-limiting beliefs
(Hello to Happiness, Adamedes, 2012.)

Unsafe

You constantly believe that you are in danger; you feel that people are trying to take advantage of you; or that you are at risk of infection.

Unworthy

You believe that you are not good enough; that you are undeserving; or that there is something wrong with you.

Alone

You find it hard to be by yourself, you find it difficult to say goodbye to loved ones, or there is no one you can depend on.

SELF-THINKING AND TALKING

How you view yourself, others and the world around you will also affect your child's view of themselves, others and the world around them.

The next section is all about happiness. We are all 100 percent in charge of creating our own happiness and being the foundation of your child's happiness. To do this, you need to be emotionally aware and able to take emotional responsibility by being open and accepting at all times of yourself, others, and circumstances that come into your everyday life. Emotional responsibility means you are in control of your mind, thoughts, and feelings.

A good example of this is to relate to a story Turia wrote on her experiences of free diving. Free diving very much involves emotional control. Basically, what happens is:

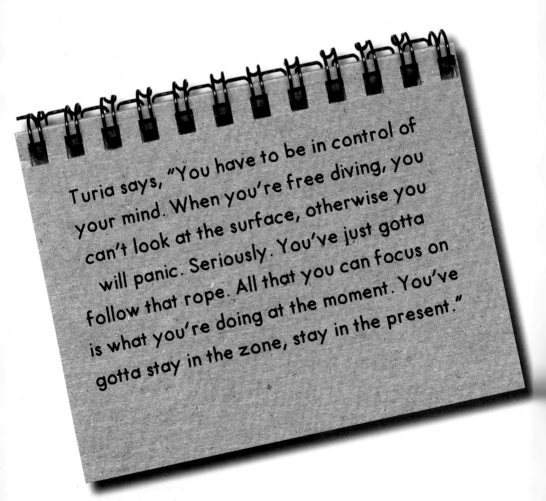

Turia says, "You have to be in control of your mind. When you're free diving, you can't look at the surface, otherwise you will panic. Seriously. You've just gotta follow that rope. All that you can focus on is what you're doing at the moment. You've gotta stay in the zone, stay in the present."

BREATH IN   **HOLD BREATH**   **BREATH OUT**

You use this technique to take you under the water all the way until you reach the bottom and then to get back up again. A technique you can use to calm yourself in everyday life.

When you are outside your comfort zone, it takes mental strength to focus and control your mind when there's no safety net.

NOTES

DR HARRY'S SHORT STORY

As long as I can remember, I have been obsessed with the ocean and what lies beneath the waves. I grew up going to the beach with my family, and I would go snorkelling at every opportunity. But I was never happy with that view from the surface. I wanted to swim down as deep as I could to look the fish in the eye!

As soon as I turned 15, I asked my parents if I could enrol in a scuba course. They were very supportive, and I loved every minute of it. As part of the course, we had to do four dives in the ocean, and the very last one was on a shipwreck a few kilometres off the coast of Adelaide.

It was a rough day, and we were in a small boat. So rough, in fact, that the other boatload of divers who were to accompany us turned back before they got to the wreck. Our skipper was a very experienced "boatie" and dive instructor, and he thought it was okay, so we carried on. We had a successful dive and surfaced at about 5 pm on a warm but windy summer's day.

Once back aboard, he turned the boat for home in a sea of waves that followed us. I remember standing up at the front of the boat next to our skipper, whooping and hollering as we raced down the back of the increasingly large waves. But the next wave was a monster, and the boat sped down the watery slope and continued into the back of the next wave, burying the front of the boat underwater, with a green wall of water crashing into my face and chest. The following wave lifted the stern of the boat up and over our heads, flipping the boat end over end. And that was it. Five of us in the water with an upturned boat and the sun soon to set.

To cut a long story short, we floated in the water for the next 14 hours until we were rescued the next morning. We clung to the boat, sometimes sitting inside it on the surface like a large bath tub until the next big wave rolled us out again. I tried not to think of the cold. I tried not to think of the sharks in the black water beneath my

44

legs. I tried not to think about how worried my parents would be. It was the longest and worst night of my life to this day.

It took me a few days to recover. I slept most of the first 36 hours! After a few days, everyone assumed I would give up diving. No way! To me this was a boating accident, and it had nothing to do with diving. And I learned so much from the mistakes we had made that I knew when one day I had my own boat, I would be safer and better on the water because of this experience. And, hey, I had a great story to tell! I have tried to find positives in any bad thing that has happened to me in my life.

If you can apply this way of thinking to everyday life and circumstances that are thrown at you — even when there are curve balls, episodes of feeling angry or hurt, or you're outside your comfort zone — you've mastered emotional responsibility.

WITH A STRIKE OF A MATCH

On September 2, 1998, the day started out as normal, well, as normal as it could be for a four-year-old. Come lunchtime, little did we know my world and my family's world was going to change significantly with the strike of a match. The flames engulfed my body, fire shooting from my head as my hair was on fire, my body and mind taken over with pain. Thrown under an outside tap, the burnt remains of my dress ripped away, and all my skin followed with it. I had full thickness burns to 40 percent of my tiny body that required hours of surgery, 83 skin grafts, synthetic skin implants, and years of rehabilitation. I was in and out of school due to follow-up appointments and months to years of hospitalisation, hidden from family and friends as a result of infection risks, learning to grow up with something "different" to everyone else, and learning to overcome the eyes that stare, the voices that whisper, and the ones that don't.

At times it seems easier to just let the bad and negative in, let the hurtful words wound, let the light slowly fade, and see the "different" as a bad thing. In 2004 on my way to a KIDS Foundation burns camp with my family, we stopped by the seaside town of Nambucca Heads to take a rest. Walking along the break wall seeing hundreds of rocks painted with names and pictures, I noticed towards the end of the wall a rock painted with a lime-green top and five simple words written on it: "Turn your scars into stars". These words resonated with me on a profound level, even then as a 10-year-old. While at camp, with these words still fresh in my mind, we were given a moment to reflect on our favourite part of the week. I painted a picture of the ocean, the rock, and those five words and gave it to Susie. From that day forward, those words have become a huge part of the KIDS Foundation, and they became my everyday mantra and a reason to look at the world in new light.

It's now been two decades since my accident, and as the people closest to me throughout my life would know, my skin doesn't faze me, nor do I let people's opinions of it faze me, either. I've now grown to see our skin as a canvas throughout our life that collects detailed pieces of unique art for a story to come together after many years. Sure, we may have a few imperfections on the base to start with, a couple of brush marks that appear throughout, but at the end of the day, no two people have a single mark that is the same, and to me that is something spectacular and beautiful. Some people would call my experience "tragic"; I see it, instead, as a life-changing opportunity.

From this experience, I've found my life passion. I've graduated from university with a Bachelor of Nursing, and for the past four years, I've been able to practise as a registered nurse, caring for those going through some of the hardest days of their lives. I've had the greatest opportunity to practise in a children's hospital that once cared for me, and even work alongside others who were there for me, during my recovery. Every day I now have the chance to influence, guide, heal, and show others that even in the hardest and darkest moments of our lives, we all have the strength to "turn our scars into stars".

BEST SELF

The best life and safety education you can give your child is to empower them to build a strong sense of identity and wellbeing. Love them, teach them to take responsibility for their emotions, and let them take managed risks like climbing monkey bars, riding bikes, and exploring our beautiful outdoors.

48

IT IS SAID THAT...

Popcorn is normally
fried in the same pot,
in the same oil,
at the same time,
at the same temperature,
but the kernels pop at different times.

All children are different;
your child's time to "pop" will happen
when they are ready.

HAPPY

Happiness is best felt when shared
with another.

You will both gain equal happiness by spending some
quality "busyness-free" time with your child, helping
them to find the things that make them feel happy.

THOUGHTS, FEELINGS AND EMOTIONS

Now, let's have a look at a thought, which is simply an idea, an idea you own. A thought is a way of thinking about a perspective you have or have chosen to adopt. Thoughts create feelings and physical sensations that stir inside your body. Love, joy, and peace are natural feelings, and on the other side fear, anger, and sadness are reactive feelings. The way you choose to think will determine the level of happiness you create — a little like the glass half-full, the glass half-empty scenario mentioned previously. Positive thoughts create positive feelings, which make you feel happy. Positive feelings are when you feel connected, safe, accepted, loved, and in control of situations.

Have you ever wondered why sometimes your thoughts are negative? Most thoughts are developed from the things in your world that surrounds you — the people you spend most of your time with, the activities you engage in, the programs you watch, and, the music you listen to. The messages you hear from all these sources transmit to your brain and become beliefs.

52

Your thoughts are mostly driven by five things you spend most of your time with or do. For example, take five people you spend most of your time with and decide whether their behaviour is more:

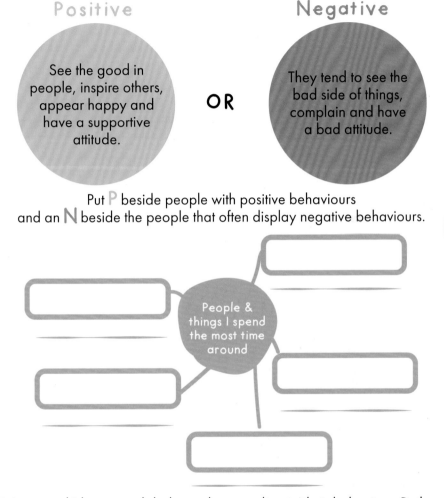

Positive

See the good in people, inspire others, appear happy and have a supportive attitude.

OR

Negative

They tend to see the bad side of things, complain and have a bad attitude.

Put P beside people with positive behaviours and an N beside the people that often display negative behaviours.

People & things I spend the most time around

HAPPY

It is a good idea not to label people according to their behaviour. Rather than referring to a person as being either negative or positive, refer to a person as having either negative or positive behaviour. Almost all people are doing their best — they are coming from limited thinking or responding to situations where they feel misunderstood or attacked.

If you surround your child with positivity, their thoughts will be empowered by this mindset. What your child thinks, feels, and believes inside will directly impact on what happens to them on the outside. Thoughts, feelings, and emotions are the things that motivate your child's behaviour and actions.

Unlike thoughts that take just a second to process, emotions take much longer to develop because they are reactive feelings that have evolved from thoughts you repeated over and over again. Many situations or events in your child's life will have an emotion attached to them. The emotional response will depend on how the child has made sense and meaning of the situation based on prior experiences, like Hakavai in the earlier section.

This also brings to mind an incident that happened to one of my grandchildren, Lewi. At the time, he had just reached 20 months of age. It was just like any other busy night in Lewi's houschold — kids coming and going. He was doing the rounds of the house on his battery-operated motorbike as he often did. The babysitter had gone downstairs to run the bath. The next thing there was an ear-piercing scream. The motorbike that Lewi was riding had caught on the corner near the stairs and sent him tumbling down the wooden staircase. A trip to the hospital revealed that other than the egg on his head, there was no other obvious damage. Now when he stands at the top of the stairs, in his own language, he tells us what happened. Lewi is now extremely cautious of the stairs. His emotional response has been caused by the pain of his staircase experience.

TAKING RESPONSIBILITY FOR EMOTIONS

Using Lewi's staircase scenario as an example, let's consider two young children learning to tackle stairs. The first child is with a parent that helps their child by either crawling down the stairs using a backward motion or skating on their bottoms with encouragement. They do this time and time again until the child has mastered the stairs and the parent has confidence that they can do it by themselves. The second child has an experience with stairs involving a fall and hurts themselves, just like Lewi.

The first child perceives the experience as rewarding, and the second child views the experience as painful and reacts differently. The same event has a completely different meaning for each child and is reflected in their entirely different emotional responses.

We all deal with emotions in our own way. The ability to take control of your emotions means that you accept what is happening and in some way detach yourself from the situation. Teaching children to practise mindfulness has been found to help them take responsibility for managing their emotions and develop the ability to self-regulate. Practising mindfulness is one way of bringing the mind and body together. It makes you present in the moment, bringing attention to what is going on, on the inside and outside of your body. Mindfulness makes you think about how you are feeling. There are considerable advantages of mindfulness that calm a child and help them to focus. With the right tools and strategies, you can help your child develop a positive mindset to drive their desired emotional response. Meditation is one way that can build a child's emotional and intellectual intelligence.

MINDFULNESS

The other day in the office we were talking about the power of mindfulness when a staff member told us this little story:

Fred came in from playing outside and was all wound up and whizzing around. I said, "Fred, calm down a bit! You're going to hurt yourself or someone." Then he turned to me and started to do the "mountain breaths". He held up one hand, spread his fingers, and with the index finger of his other hand, he ran it up and down his outspread fingers, taking a breath in on the up action and a breath out on the down. And when he had finished, he said, "I'm all better now; I do that at kinder when we get a little crazy." And then he walked off and started playing with his Lego. He was calm.

Mindfulness is being aware and noticing our thoughts; how our body is feeling; what our eyes are seeing; what our ears are hearing; and being of aware anything else that is around us and happening right now.

MINDFULNESS—MEDITATION

One form of mindfulness is meditation. If you can find just five minutes per day to practise some form of meditation, it will help to keep your child calm.

- Choose the type of meditation that works best for your child.

- Practise deep breathing or other forms of relaxation as part of your child's daily bedtime routine.

- Ideas for meditation can be found in books, videos, on websites, or through smartphone apps.

- Calming background music can be useful in setting the mood.

- Create a mantra with your child. The mantra could be something like: "I am happy, I am safe, I am special, I am ME."

Start your child's day with a positive thought that you create together like:

- Today is going to be awesome.
- Today, both of us are going to do something special for someone.
- Today, we are going to smile as much as we can.

MEDITATION IDEAS
- Breath – mountain breaths (like Fred)
- Breath – numbers, shapes and objects
- Cloud or star-gazing – on a clear night even if it means rugging up
- Bird-watching
- Storytelling or painting the visual picture
- Cuddle friends (using soft textured toy for cuddling)
- Eye pillows
- Listening to sounds or music
- Yoga for children – for example, Cosmic kids yoga
- Mindful eating
- Mantras

MEDITATION

Meditation has been used since ancient times to improve health and wellbeing. It's a time when your child can take time out. Teaching your child how to stop, focus, and breathe will help them to relax and function more effectively and clearly. Resting the mind and body has many benefits for mental and physical health. These days there are more and more studies being conducted in school settings that include meditation sessions in their daily routine, and they have demonstrated that there are real benefits from the practice. Results have shown improved behaviour, reduced anxiety and depression, and better sleeping patterns, as well as improved physical and mental performance. If you choose to practise meditation with your child, it means you are present and in the moment with them.

Many meditation practices include breathing techniques to encourage calmness. The practice could simply involve mountain breathing like Fred, or sitting quietly with closed eyes and thinking about their breath. For some children, sitting quietly for any length of time can be quite challenging. There are also other options such as movement-based meditation, using mantras, or even yoga.

THINGS THAT MAKE YOU HAPPY

Happiness has the same ingredients, but it varies for everyone. You own your own happiness. No one can tell you what your happiness is or what makes happiness for you. When you find it, you own it, it is inside you and surrounds you. Happiness is equally available to everyone because it is free. What makes your child happy will have a totally different meaning than your happiness. If you think money will buy you happiness, you will never be satisfied, because happiness is not just a materialistic thing.

Think really carefully about your definition of happiness as it will influence every other significant decision in your life. If you are aware of the happiness that you already have, you will begin to experience more happiness around you. This will have a flow-on effect to your child.

Now let's think about things that make you truly happy, like:

the people that love you,

your friends,

physical things like exercise,

listening to music,

things that make you laugh,

kindness,

the warmth of the sun,

being stress free,

a warm bath,

staring at the stars at night.

What makes your child happy?

It is important that you do not push your ideas of happiness on to your child. What you think might make them happy may not actually be what makes them happy. Let them tell you, and talk to them about it so that you really understand.

Create a happy board

You may like to either draw or cut and paste pictures to make a happy board with the things that make them happy. Even frame it or put it in a book so that they can refer to it when they are feeling not so happy. Explain to your child that they may not always be happy all the time and that is okay.

Happiness senses

Senses are things that can make you happy. A great senses activity to do with your child is to select a place where you and your child can consciously experience senses. Find a comfy place, like a courtyard or garden, to sit and relax on a seat, the grass, or lie on a beanbag.

Instruct your child to close their eyes, then ask them:
- What can you hear?
- What can you smell?
- How do the sounds make you feel?
- What do you see/imagine when you close your eyes?

MY HAPPY PLACE

In Chapter 3, in the Safe section, we also talk about "happy places and safety zones", but with a focus on the importance of relationship boundaries. In this happy section, "My Happy Place", the attention is given to things that make your child happy, which may include being with another person.

Another activity to do with your child together is to draw a visual representation of their happy place. It could be their home, their kindergarten, a cubby house, or even a holiday destination, or, like Harry, a diving cave.

HAPPY PLACE

FEELING UNHAPPY

If you're not feeling very happy about yourself, here are 10 things you can try...

1. Look at the reasons WHY you are not happy.

2. What can you learn from this experience or situation? Is there something you can change, or how can you grow from it?

3. Accept that you may not always be happy all the time.

4. Accept that you will have good days and bad days. Tomorrow is a new day, and you will probably feel better then.

5. Take responsibility for your own happiness.

6. Start practising gratitude.

7. Clean up your social media feed with friends that have good messages or people that inspire you.

8. Get a mantra like "I may feel bad today, but I won't always feel this way."

9. List your small wins.

10. Pick something from your "Happy" list and do it.

Ways to help your child deal with situations of unhappiness could be to:

- ask them why they are not happy
- ask them what do they think they can learn from this experience
- ask them if there is something they could change
- explain to them that they may not always be happy all the time
- explain to them that they will have good days and bad days and that tomorrow is a new day and they will probably feel better
- get them to think of something that may be related to the situation that they may be grateful for
- say a mantra like "I may feel sad today, but I won't always feel this way"
- get your child to go to the "Happy Board" you have made with them
- get your child to pick something from their "Happy Board" and think about it.

CONFIDENCE

Another thing that can bring happiness is having confidence. Confidence begins with positive self-belief and personal power — a state of being authentic and true to your values and integrity. Explain to your child that having confidence is believing you can do a particular thing, a feel-good doing thing.

An activity you can do with your child:

Create a feel good/confidence star with your child by putting in each of the five star arms the things that give your child the feel good/confidence feeling like:

- The people they like being around and who make them feel happy — family members, friends, or even pets.
- Physical activities they like doing — riding a trike/bike, playing with their dog, futsal.
- Kinder – playdough, painting, playing games.
- Places they like going to – beach, pool, playground.
- Appearance – having their hair done or wearing nice clothes or their favourite shoes.

Having confidence to say or do something can make your child feel happy. An example of this for an adult could be when you put a post on social media and you get a "like"; it may give you a little ego boost. Which is okay, but such things shouldn't be the only way you feel good about yourself. One of the dangers is that you're relying on what other people think about you to make you feel good, and your confidence has got to come from within.

Excerpt from Turia Pitt. *Good Selfie*, Apple Books

When a child believes their emotions are understood, their behaviour changes and uncontrollable emotions begin to disperse. If you can stay calm and not get pulled into the battle, you are actually acting as a great role model. When your child takes control of the situation, feelings of competence and power emerge. This is a good time to empower the problem-solving gene by resisting the urge to do it for them. Encourage them instead by showing you have confidence in their ability to handle the situation. Tackling manageable challenges with your assistance will give your child the confidence to try new things, develop further, and take the next step. In the academic world, they call this "scaffolding". You do this by encouraging them to take mini steps one step at a time, building their competence, self-satisfaction, and confidence.

This is the real letting-go stage for a parent. Be there to support them, but don't do it for them. You will find that you are holding their hands less and less.

Explain to your child that you don't always feel confident about doing certain things and that's okay. Another not-feeling-confident thing is being self-conscious about something. Explain to your child that you and everyone else experiences self-consciousness at times and that's okay, too.

Provide some ideas of little things they can do to overcome not feeling confident that works for them, such as:

• If it is a physical thing like riding a bike, teach them how and give them lots of practice until it becomes natural to them and the lack of confidence slowly fades.

• Get them to do something that makes them feel good, something from their happy list or confidence star.

Confidence is such a big part of the happiness picture.

LOVE

To be happy yourself, you have to be the most loving person you can be. For your child to be truly happy, they need to feel the love you feel for them. By giving quality time, energy, and attention to your child, you will both experience more happiness. One of our most important relationships we have is with our child, but so often it has to compete with our busyness, and the busyness often wins. Let's make a conscious effort to stop some of the busyness and think about how you could spend more time with them and be grateful for having them in your life to have more time and fun with.

One of the greatest things you can give your child to help them get to know there own self is love.

Convey love by showing and telling your child you love them and that they are loved. Help your child to truly understand the abundance of love they have in their lives. Allow your child the right to choose the form of affection they like. Being cuddled and kissed is okay if your child is okay with it. They will soon let you or others know if it is not, provided they are taught about personal safety. Parents who stop behaving affectionately with their children themselves may end up conveying the message that physical affection is not normal. Being hugged shows a child that they are loved and have been seen and acknowledged. Children need human interaction to feel that they belong.

Ideas for sharing love:

- Give them lots of hugs so that they feel loved, seen, and valued.
- Tell them often that you love them.
- Bend down and make eye contact when sharing your feelings with them.
- Tell them you will always be there for them.
- Create a little saying with actions that you can share with your child that reinforces love like:

"I love you" (point to yourself and then your child)

"You love me" (point to your child and then yourself)

"We are a loving family" (then give your child a hug)

- Write a simple love note or draw a picture and leave it in an unexpected place like in the pocket of their jacket or under their pillow.
- Place a special family photo or a photo of you and your child and leave it in their kinder bag.
- Make a keepsake box together, where your child can put your love notes, photos, or meaningful items like a shell from a holiday or a crystal.

Some of the greatest things you can give your child to help them get to know their own self is love, time, opportunity to make choices, and a wealth of experiences.

WHAT ARE YOU GRATEFUL FOR?

Gratitude is also a part of our happiness. Being grateful for someone or something and acknowledging it is a real good feeling. When you feel gratitude, you're grateful for what someone did for you or for what has happened. Talk to your child about gratitude and get them to think about the things that they are grateful for. It could be a person in their life, something someone did for them, or an attribute they have, like great swimming ability. Talk about their strengths, things they are good at. Make a "This is ME book", where you can enter all the activities that you do with your child and devote some space to writing a list of their strengths.

I'M GRATEFUL FOR:
✓ All of my friends.
✓ My warm cosy bed.
✓ My loving parents.
✓ The food in our pantry.
✓ All of my toys.
✓ The weekends.
✓ My bike.
✓ Rainy and sunny days.

GOALS

Teaching children to set goals from an early age can help them establish a foundation for greater goals and opportunities for later in their lives. When helping your child to set goals, you need them to be clear about what it is that they really want to achieve or are wanting to do, so that you can help them to achieve it with limited input but good guidance.

Ideas to get them started:

1. Talk about something they really want to achieve or do. For example, ride a bike.

2. Talk to them about what they might need to achieve their goal.

3. Help them to break the goal into small steps. For example, "Let's start with training wheels."

4. Bring in your commitment to help.

5. Get them to take tiny progressive steps so they will eventually get there and do it on their own.

6. Show them that you believe they can do it so that they also gain self-belief.

7. Reward them along the way. For example, "You're such a good rider."

8. Give them opportunities for lots of practice so they can improve and gain self-pride. Tell them how far they have come each time. For example, "Look at you balancing."

9. Tell them they can do this. For example, "You can do this now without my help."

10. When they have achieved their goal, tell them you are so proud of them for trying so hard and achieving what they started out to do. For example, "I'm so proud of you. You wanted to ride a bike and now you are doing it all by yourself."

GOAL SETTING AND MONEY SAVING

At the same time you are teaching your child about goal setting, you may like to bring in teaching them about money. Children are often fascinated by money and how it works. You could start by talking about the different coins and notes and their values. Maybe use cash at the pay counters to show the process of handing over money in exchange for goods. When withdrawing money from an ATM, explain that the money coming out is not a magic hole in the wall that spits out money when you need it, it is actually coming out of your bank account.

If you think your child is up to goal setting, money not only provides a great opportunity to achieve an attainable aim but it is also great for teaching gratification and appreciation — the earn and reward concept.

Inspiration on money goal setting comes straight from the bestselling author Scott Pape's second book, *The Barefoot Investor for FAMILIES: The Only Kids' Money Guide You'll Ever Need.*

Like anything in life, you need to tailor things to make it work for you, your child, and your family. We've altered it to suit our grandkids' holiday visits, when we all get together. There are 17 of us and one on the way, all in the same house. Tying jobs in with pocket money makes it workable and means everyone is engaged, and it is one of the occasions we have together when we get to have non-digital time.

Using a spend, save and share concept helps children to appreciate money in a rewarding way. They can spend a little for an instant reward, work hard to save for something they really want, and then experience the pleasure sharing brings by helping someone less fortunate. There are commercial 'spend, save and share' money box systems like the moonjar or you might like to make your own from bottles or jars.

JOBS CHART

You may like to create a chart with a jobs list that the children tick to reach their goals to receive their pocket money. Having something to work towards encourages your child to continue to save.

JOBS CHART	MON	TUES	WED	THUR	FRI	SAT	SUN
Job 1							
Job 2							
Job 3							
Job 4							
Job 5							
Job 6							

I'M SAVING FOR...

_____

_____

_____

_____

PASTE A PICTURE OF
WHAT YOUR CHILD IS
SAVING FOR HERE:

SPEND, SAVE AND SHARE

An example to follow:

1. Find a picture of the thing that they are saving for, like the ball on the previous page, and paste it into the space provided on the chart.

2. Agree on the steps they need to take — if, for example, the ball costs $20, you may say, "Let's go halves; if you save $10, I will pay $10."

3. Decide on jobs that are expected of them without financial reward and the jobs they can do to gain their pocket money. For example:

- Set the table
- Feed the dog (if you have one)
- Water the plants
- Make their bed
- Help to tidy up or clean
- Recycle
- Wash, dry, or put away the dishes

It is best to set small goals so that they can achieve it within days or a few weeks and not lose enthusiasm.

4. Give them their three money bottles. On pocket-money day, they separate their pocket money into the three bottles so that they can see what they are achieving.

5. Provide lots of encouragement and reward them for a great job.

6. Count the money with them at the end of each week.

7. When they finally reach their $10 goal in the save bottle, they are ready to purchase their goal ball.

8. Involve your child in going to the store and purchasing their ball.

Scott's book is now used at the KIDS Foundation injury and trauma recovery camps to inspire our younger participants on how to manage money and set financial goals.

MATT'S STORY

The Barefoot Investor for Families may not have been around when Matt was young; however, we guess his parents instilled some of Scott's principles in order to raise such a well-grounded, beautifully natured young person who in turn has inspired many and given them the will to live.

Matt is now a confident, happy young man who has started his own business setting up vending machines in corporate office buildings. He has also moved into the house he helped to build, where he actually contributed manually to its construction.

Matt was trapped in a car fire in April 1999 at the age of three. He sustained full-thickness burns to just over 30 percent of his body, with the worst of his burns being to his face, head, and hands. He spent three-and-a-half months in hospital and 33 days in intensive care. After two cardiac arrests, the doctors suggested that his life support be switched off, but he fought on hard. Matt has been on a tough and emotional journey but is not one to feel sorry for himself. When Matt came to the KIDS Foundation at 10 years of age, he was shy and thought he was the only person that had ever been burnt. But Matt soon learnt that there were many other survivors with stories similar to his and even some more devastating. Matt believes the KIDS Foundation has been lifechanging for him: "People often stare; I would too; they're only curious, so I just smile and it makes their stares worthwhile."

People often stare; I would too; they're only curious, so I just smile and it makes their stares worthwhile.

Matt is a youth ambassador for the KIDS Foundation. He has an inspirational story, and his changed appearance attracts many stares, but he has the best attitude.

HEALTHY

Being healthy means you are physically and mentally well and bounce back from sickness, injuries, or being able to manage other problems.

The things that contribute to good health include your genes, relationships, the environment, and education.

The environment includes places where children live, play, and grow. Healthy environments include clean air and water, nutritious food, and green spaces to play and explore.

You often hear that healthy things sometimes cost you more than unhealthy things. Actually, seven out of the eight most important things for your child's health cost very little if anything at all.

HEALTHY VALUES

1 AIR — BREATHING IT

2 WATER — DRINKING IT

3 WHOLEFOODS — EATING THEM

4 EXERCISE — DOING IT

5 SUNSHINE — GETTING OUTDOORS

6 SLEEP — PLENTY OF IT

7 RELATIONSHIPS — HAVING POSITIVE ONES

8 HYGIENE — KEEPING CLEAN

1. AIR— BREATHING IT

Breathing and doing it properly is one of the most important things in being healthy!

Breathing — we all do it, but most of us aren't even aware of it and how important it is to our moods, anxiety, and health. In an earlier section, we talked about breathing and the benefits of meditation. In this chapter, it is more about the physical benefits. One of the most important things you can do for your child's health is to teach them to breathe properly.

A bit of information on breathing in case you haven't given it much thought ... It does sound crazy, but most people don't think about how they breathe and tend to shallow breathe. After we inhale, the oxygen from the air is absorbed across the thin membranes in the lungs and into the bloodstream. The red blood cells then carry the oxygen to the tissues where it is used to produce energy. Exhaling does the opposite — breathing out expels the waste product, which is carbon dioxide. Breathing properly means you need to breathe deeply into the lower part of your lungs.
You can do this by breathing through your nose—it slows the air coming in and helps with relaxation.

There are many other benefits of breathing properly. It:

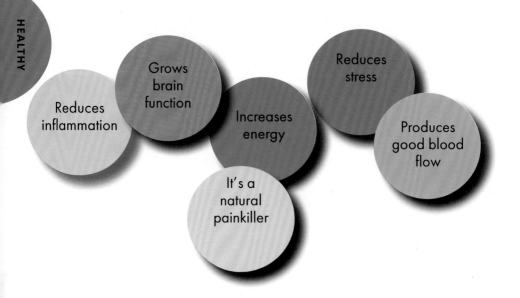

Reduces inflammation

Grows brain function

Reduces stress

Increases energy

Produces good blood flow

It's a natural painkiller

HEALTHY

Try this: Find a place that you and your child can get into a relaxed state and think about how you are breathing.

- How many seconds does it take you to breathe in?
- How many to breathe out?
- Is the pattern steady?
- Does your abdomen move each time you and your child breathe?
- Is the breathing pattern even?

Think about the above breathing technique, doing it deeply and slowly when relaxed. Feel it moving into the abdomen area and filling the lungs with each breath in. This is proper breathing.

Proper breathing

If you watch a baby, you will notice that they breathe properly. A great breathing activity to do with your child is relaxed "proper breathing". Ask your child to pretend their belly is like a balloon, push all the air right to the end of the balloon, and when you breathe out, it releases.

Start out with 3 seconds and work your way up!

INHALE 3 SECS	HOLD 3 SECS	EXHALE 3 SECS	HOLD 3 SECS
INHALE 5 SECS	HOLD 5 SECS	EXHALE 5 SECS	HOLD 5 SECS
INHALE 7 SECS	HOLD 7 SECS	EXHALE 7 SECS	HOLD 7 SECS

Plants give you oxygen

You probably haven't thought much about the health benefits of having real plants in your home. It has been said that certain plants clean air and filter out toxins. You may like to teach your child about a few of the plants that are known to clean up indoor air like the following plants — Mother-in-Law's Tongue, Areca Palm, and Peace Lily.

Mother-in-Law's Tongue

This plant will thrive under most conditions. It is said to convert carbon dioxide to oxygen at night. Three of these waist-high plants is a good idea in the bedroom.

Areca Palm

It is said that the Areca Palm is supposed to remove xylene and toluene from the air, but it also happens to convert carbon dioxide to oxygen during the daytime. Having four shoulder-high plants of these per person in your household apparently provides enough oxygen to survive on during daylight hours!

Peace Lily

The Peace Lily is known for removing air pollutants. This plant can be kept in mid-light to shade.

If having live plants in the home is something you would like to do, take a trip with your child to the local nursery and purchase a few of these plants together. It could even be your child's job to water and care for them so they gain an understanding that plants are living things.

Other ways to clean the air:

Open up the doors and windows in your house for 10–20 minutes each day.

- Roll down the window in your car to let the air circulate.
- Turn on a ceiling or standard fan to circulate the air.

2. WATER— DRINKING IT

Water has so many benefits. It's good for you and doesn't really cost much. The best fluid you can encourage your child to drink is water. Why? Because it...

- hydrates your body
- regulates your body temperature
- delivers oxygen around your body
- helps your skin, joints, and muscles stay soft and supple
- helps the healing process by bringing in nutrients and taking away waste.

Water is the foundation of good health. To become healthier, encourage your child to drink water more often.

There are many ways to source water. The most commonly is from the tap, which is relatively free, or you can pay for bottled water.

Sources of water

- Spring water
- Filtered water
- Ionised water
- Alkaline water (alkaline water bottle, alkaline jug filters)
- Bottled water
- Tap water

Another great benefit of water is that it stops you feeling hungry, therefore, you don't want to eat as much. So let's start drinking enough water each day to satisfy your thirst. Also drinking plenty of water helps you feel, sleep, and heal better.

HEALTHY

3. WHOLEFOODS — EATING THEM

Wholefoods are not only good for you but they are also the best source of nourishment for healthy children. Wholefoods are basically fruit and veggies. There are many ways of preparing and giving wholefoods to children that are fun and yummy.

This third health value is probably the most expensive, but, in a lot of cases, we eat more than we need. So, by eating less but more of the good foods, you may not break the budget. Wholefoods are foods that are whole and haven't been "messed around with" – basically fruit, vegetables, nuts, and seeds. We are big believers of incorporating as much raw food into kids' diets as possible for all the great health reasons.

Fun with wholefoods
You can do some fun things with wholefoods like making faces on plates or cutting shapes, figures, or animals from the fruits and vegetables. There are heaps of ideas on the internet for inspiration, and you can involve your child, helping them to grow their imagination.

Seasonal fruit and vegetables

Seasonal fruit and vegetables are the best. You don't need to go deep into the science and benefits of individual fruits and vegetables; you could simply talk about carrots as being good for their eyes and make a vegie face with carrot eyes, a fruit or vegie stick figure, or maybe in the shape of a person.

Other great ways of consuming wholefoods are through juices and smoothies.

Fun snacks

Cut raw veggies (carrots, broccoli, peppers, celery, cauliflower, cucumber) to use with a dip (hummus, nut cream). Put out fruit (apples, pears, bananas, oranges, etc.) and nuts so that your kids can have them when they're hungry.

Whole means "complete".
When something is complete,
it is not lacking or deficient.

SOME OF OUR LITTLE-PEOPLE FAVOURITES:

BERRY YUM

Ingredients:
1 cup of blueberries
6 raspberries
4 strawberries cut up
6 blackberries
6 dark-choc-coated goji berries (optional treat)
1 tablespoon of coconut yoghurt (vanilla bean Coyo)

Directions:
Tip the cup of blueberries into a dessert bowl.
Add the remaining fruit and coconut yoghurt, stir and serve.

HEALTHY

CHOC MINT NICE CREAM

Ingredients:

1 frozen banana
1 small cup of ice
1 cup of vanilla bean Coyo yoghurt
40g raw almonds
3 drops of food-grade peppermint oil
1 cup of finely chopped fresh mint leaves

40g raw cashews
2 tbs organic cacao powder
6 finely chopped dates
1 teaspoon of Manuka honey

Method:

1. In a food processor, blend the nuts until they are grounded and powdery looking.

2. Add the frozen banana, ice, yoghurt, dates, cacao powder, honey, peppermint oil, and mint leaves into the processor and blend until smooth.

3. Pour into an airtight container and put into the freezer.

4. It is best to remove from the freezer five minutes before serving so as to soften it a little.

YUM PUM SOUP

Ingredients:
Med/large butternut pumpkin
Vegetable stock (if you are not making your own, check the ingredients do not contain artificial sweeteners, hydrogenated oils, gelatine, MSG artificial colours, pesticides, and GMO)
6 sticks of lemon grass
400ml can of organic coconut milk
2 bunches of finely chopped coriander

Method:
1. Chop up the pumpkin and place into a saucepan.
2. Add stock and bring to the boil.
3. Reduce heat and add lemongrass sticks, whole but bent in half to bring out the flavour.
4. Simmer for 20 minutes.
5. Remove lemongrass.
6. Add finely chopped coriander.
7. Add coconut milk.
8. Mix with a blender.
9. Serve with a sprinkle of coriander on top.

YUM PUM NOODLES

Ingredients:
Pumpkin soup from previous night
2 medium-sized zucchinis, shredded into noodles or other noodles of your choice
300g of fresh podded peas
Parmesan cheese

Method:
Boil a pot of water, add the zucchini, or other noodles of your choice, and cook for one minute.
Drain the noodles in a colander and serve into bowls.
Put pumpkin sauce and peas into a saucepan, place on the stove, and heat gradually for five minutes (peas should still be quite raw).
Pour pumpkin and pea sauce over the top of the zucchini noodles. Your choice if you would like to add a tablespoon of parmesan cheese.

4. EXERCISE — DOING IT

Walking

Walking is the simplest, cheapest, and most convenient way to exercise with your child. Walking is not only a fun thing to do for exercise, it is also a great time to explore beautiful places, for socialising and learning, and spending time with your dog if you have one.

Bike-riding

Another great exercise to do with your child is to go on a bike ride. Bike-riding is a form of exercise that involves a skill. It can be a little more restricting because, depending on where you live, your yard may be small and bike paths and parks may not be in close proximity. However, bike-riding has some of the same benefits as walking like exploring places, socialising, and learning a new skill.

Swimming

Teach your child to swim. Take them to swimming lessons, or even free play at a water park.

Sport

Enrol your child in modified team sports like Auskick or Futsal. Or let them participate in individual sports or skill development activities, like gymnastics or ballet.

Play

Play is a fun way to exercise with your child. Role-play in your home. For example, playing ball games in the backyard or taking them to a playground.

Play is another way to exercise
with your child.

5. SUNSHINE — GETTING OUTDOORS

Sunshine makes you feel happy...

Believe it or not, sunshine is actually good for your child. So, take them outside and let them enjoy it, but be sensible about it as children burn easily, and sunburn at a young age can be associated with causing unhealthy skin conditions later in life. When the days get warmer, you can have fun outdoor activities, like going on a hike, riding a bike, taking up outdoor sport, going to the beach, or planning a camping trip. You will be surprised to see how much getting outdoors and spending time being active can do for your health. Sunny days actually have some pretty amazing health benefits.

Spending time outside, early morning or later in the day, helps to avoid the harshest rays. Most of us have grown up with the catchphrase "Slip, slop, slap": slip on a shirt, slop on sunscreen, and slap on a hat. If you do spend a lot of time in the direct sun, protecting your skin during the times when the sun is at its hottest and the rays harshest is very important. You can do this by finding a shaded spot, wearing a hat and a t-shirt, and applying a good-quality sunscreen.

There is an app called *Chemical Maze*, which you can download to help you understand what chemicals are in products and foods. Read the labels. There are sunscreens available that use more natural additives, and it would be wise to look into the best available for you and your family.

HEALTHY

6. SLEEP — GETTING IT

How much sleep is enough? Just like everything else we have discussed, every child is different – some need more sleep, and others need less. The ideal sleep time for four- to six-year-olds is a solid 10 to 13 hours each night.

You can help them to develop good sleeping habits by having a consistent bedtime routine, like setting a suitable time to go to bed and sticking to it every night.

HEALTHY

If your child has trouble falling asleep or wakes up often in the night, here are some tips for a better night's sleep:

Suitable bedtime
7:30 pm
A regular bedtime helps a child's internal clock stay on track and helps them to fall asleep easily and quickly.

Bedtime routine
Have a bath or shower
Put on PJs
Say a mantra
Tell or read a story
Turn lights out

You may, initially, like to give your child a special sticker for getting into bed when you ask them so they have some incentive to get through the rest of the routine. If you find your bedtime routine dragging on longer than you would like, take steps to trim it back – one book or story, but not book after book.

Big bed
If your child hasn't moved to a big bed, it's probably time if that works for you.

Something special
A special cuddly soft toy might be just the thing they need to give them the "I'm safe in bed" feeling.

Goodnight hug, kiss and tuck-in
Give your child a hug and goodnight kiss, and then tuck them in.

HEALTHY

7. RELATIONSHIPS — HAVING POSITIVE ONES

Relationships can bring the most joy and the most pain. Surround yourself and your child in ones that make you feel good. It is said that after the need for water, food, and shelter, having relationships and being connected to others is the greatest emotional human need. With love and affection comes happiness. It's so important for your child to feel they are loved because your child then also gets to feel valued, appreciated, and happy. This is talked about more in the "Happy" section.

Primary psychological needs
- The need to belong
- The need to feel special and unique

10 tips for building a healthy relationship with your child
1. Loving yourself and being comfortable with who you are means you will be a happier parent.
2. Provide unconditional love.
3. Be affectionate.
4. Communicate and be present.
5. Be honest.
6. Have compassion.
7. Give encouragement.
8. Forgive and ask for forgiveness.
9. Give each other some space.
10. Provide support and commitment.
11. Give yourself at least one hour of "me time".
12. Look after your health and sleep.

Be accepting of your child the way they are

Ideas for helping your child to build healthy relationships with others

The starting point is to teach your child to have a good relationship with their "self". Understanding who they are is a building block to the following:

Teach them:

8. HYGIENE — KEEPING CLEAN

Another feel-good thing that keeps your child healthy is good personal hygiene. It will help boost their confidence and self-esteem and help to kill germs to avoid getting sick.

Good personal hygiene practices:

1. Wash your hands as much as possible, for at least 20 seconds:
   - after you go to the toilet
   - before you eat
   - every time you touch a pet

2. Have regular baths or showers.

3. Brush and floss your teeth.

4. Cough, sneeze, or yawn into a tissue or your elbow.

A little sneezing rhyme to share...

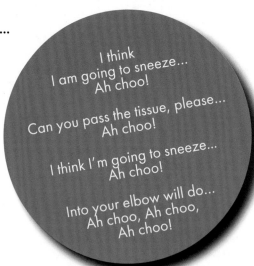

I think
I am going to sneeze...
Ah choo!

Can you pass the tissue, please...
Ah choo!

I think I'm going to sneeze...
Ah choo!

Into your elbow will do...
Ah choo, Ah choo,
Ah choo!

Fresh clothes and clean underwear every day is especially important, even if their clothes aren't smelly. Kindergarten or preschool uniforms, if they have them, especially winter over-garments, are a bit tricky to wash daily. When they get home each day, you can hang up their uniform to air to help keep up the freshness.

SAFE

Your child's safety is sure to be one of the things on your worry list. And, yes, it is your job to keep your child safe. But it is also your job as a supporter to make sure you give your child heaps of different experiences and opportunities where they get to make their own decisions about the things they can do for themselves.

This does not mean throwing them into the big wide world and seeing if they can make it on their own. It means guiding them in a way that allows them to develop understanding of the situation and letting them make choices that contribute to the activity and world around them.

SAFETY

If you google the meaning of safety, it usually reads something like "little risk of no injury." Weigh up the odds if your child asks to do something you really don't want them to do. Before you say "no", ask yourself, "By letting them do this, can they hurt themselves or could someone else get hurt?" and if the answer is "no", then why not let them do it?

Safety and risk understanding is so much a personal thing because it links to what you are capable of, your knowledge, and your experiences. What is a risk to one child may be safe to another due to their situation, just as the same situation may be experienced differently by different children.

SAFE

Letting them make decisions and giving choices to do things may be one of the most useful tools you can give your child. Feelings of mastery and capability are about power and strength driven from a child's experience of succeeding and making a difference. The more they see themselves as capable, the more likely they are to push themselves through challenges, to keep trying, to practise things, to improve, and to learn that there are personal rewards through achievements.

Too much risk can put your child in danger. Alternatively, too little risk can prevent them from gaining valuable human qualities like:

Experiencing rewards from achievements

Building confidence in their own judgment

Developing a sense of security and freedom

Gaining confidence to participate

Claiming their independence

Losing

Experiencing consequences of their actions

Gaining emotional satisfaction

Knowing their limits

Understanding what their capabilities are

SAFE

The train that can

I have memories of my mum showing me a little movie of *The Train That Can*. In the story, the train is trying to get up the hill and talks itself into it by repeating, "I think I can, I think I can, I think I can, I know I can." Maybe see if you can find a copy on the internet and show it to them.

There are other encouragement sayings like:

- Practice makes perfect.
- If you don't succeed, try, try again.
- Follow your dreams.
- Reach for the stars.
- The sky is the limit.
- If you don't give it a go, you will never know.

GOING TO "BIG" KINDERGARTEN OR PRESCHOOL

Going to "big" kindergarten or preschool might be the first time your child has been away from you with people they may not know so well. This big step into their independent world sometimes causes a bit of anxiety about being separated from you for a period of time. This is called separation anxiety.

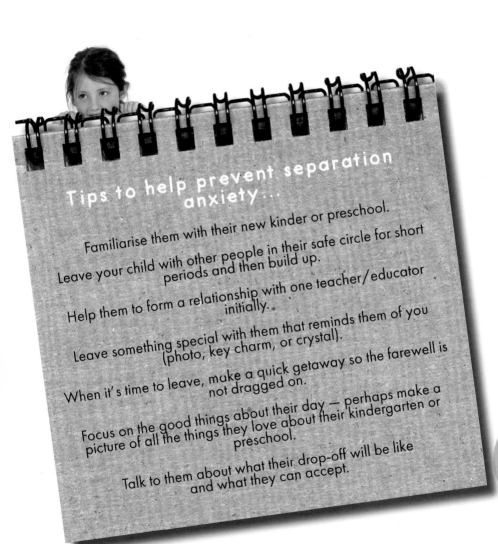

Tips to help prevent separation anxiety...

Familiarise them with their new kinder or preschool.

Leave your child with other people in their safe circle for short periods and then build up.

Help them to form a relationship with one teacher/educator initially.

Leave something special with them that reminds them of you (photo, key charm, or crystal).

When it's time to leave, make a quick getaway so the farewell is not dragged on.

Focus on the good things about their day — perhaps make a picture of all the things they love about their kindergarten or preschool.

Talk to them about what their drop-off will be like and what they can accept.

WHEN BAD THINGS HAPPEN

At different times, major events happen that appear on TV, people talk about them, and your child may ask about them. For example, the Bali bombings, the Dreamworld incident, the Thai cave rescue, the Australian bushfires, and more recently, COVID-19, have been big events that have affected many Australians and others around the world. Such events may affect your child, especially if your child is sensitive. It's important to talk to your child about them in appropriate language and talk about what happened. Keep it simple, not too ghastly; we don't want them to be fearful of their world. These events could cause your child to create an irrational perspective of the big wide world. Ask them how they are feeling. Explain that this is a bad thing and sometimes bad things happen to good people. Help them to understand that these things are very rare, but when they happen, there are so many good people that can help. Maybe you can help by giving your time, supporting a person that has been involved in the event, or even donate to the cause, and turn the focus on the good things that come out of those bad situations.

Here are some steps to take

- Acknowledge feelings.
- Talk – discuss thoughts.
- Rationalise the situation.
- Help if you can.
- Give them hope – focus on the good.
- Return them to their happy world.

SAFETY AND VIRUSES

When virus pandemics occur, like COVID-19, it brings sadness and challenges to many, but also opportunity and change for everyone. Our everyday world changes in response to the advice and direction being provided by the authorities that monitor these situations as they evolve and the authorities respond appropriately. Because these viruses can be transmitted from person to person through coughing and sneezing, the government puts in place rules to try to stop the virus spreading. During these times, we all have to adapt to work within the parameters and guidelines to ensure we stay as safe and as well as we can.

Your child will be trying to understand what is happening and will most probably notice changes in you and those closest to them. Kids are like sponges — they soak up what they hear from you, TV, radio, and friends at kinder or preschool.

When these events occur, it is important to help your child make sense of what is happening and what they are experiencing. It is important that they feel they are safe:

• Find the right time to talk with your child.

• Listen to what they have to say and the questions they ask.

• Ask about how your child is feeling and what they are experiencing at home and at kindergarten or preschool.

• Ask them if anything has been worrying them.

• Be conscious of what is being shown on the television while your child is present in the room, and restrict programs that focus only on the negative side of the situation.

• Try to keep your child's daily routine as normal as possible. Explain that sometimes we can't do the things we normally do, like going to a playground, but we can go for a walk or have lots of fun in our own yards, even if they are small. For example; cooking, crafts, nature walks.

SAFE

- Explain that sometimes these viruses can make people feel sick, but there are lots of good people that work really hard to help them get well for example, doctors and nurses.

- Explain to your child that when there is a virus that is very catchy like COVID-19 or the flu, we need to protect older people. Sometimes it is best not to visit them just in case you have the virus hiding inside you because you don't want it to pass on to them. It's really important though to try to stay connected with loved ones, especially our grandparents, at times that require us to stay away like this. Calling via phone or video, sending photos, or creating artwork or making something to send to them to let them know you are thinking of them are some ideas.

1.5m distance

SAFE

Discuss with your child how important it is that we all do our bit to help stop spread the virus; even little people can do their bit to help.

Some examples

Wash your hands after you go to the toilet, before you eat, every time you touch a pet and as much as possible for at least 20 seconds.

Stay healthy by eating good foods, drink lots of water and exercise.

Remember to think of ways to let your loved ones know you care when you can't be with them.

Cough, sneeze or yawn into a tissue or your elbow.

Use social distancing when necessary – maybe use a wave or blow a kiss.

SAFE

DANGER

Making decisions about safety is very much about taking a common-sense attitude. One of your greatest challenges as a parent is to find a balanced and practical approach to managing what are real and perceived dangers. Places that we considered fun are often now connected to places of "danger." Trees, playgrounds, monkey bars, sandpits – we can't remember these as dangers as a child. To us, they were places of fun and adventure. Weigh up the odds of benefits versus risks, and question yourself about whether it is a real or perceived danger.

REAL AND PERCEIVED DANGERS

The news will expose you to stories of child abuse, missing children, and kidnappings. Don't get "the terrifieds" and become paranoid about letting your child out of your sight. The fact is most of the harm done to children is committed by people they know. Five percent of sexual assault cases are related to "stranger danger", and in 70 percent to 90 percent of cases, the offender is known to them. The majority of child kidnappings are committed by parents or guardians, not strangers. We need to teach our children that most strangers are good, but occasionally a stranger is not a safe person to be with, so it's best not to go anywhere with them.

Giving your child age-appropriate information about the right to feel safe around body ownership provides them with tools to recognise different kinds of feelings and how to manage them. Remember we talked about feelings in earlier sections and that they come from environments and unconsciousness. If your child can understand the unsafe or unsure situation feeling, whether it be personal or physical safety, it is important they know what to do next and when to get help.

Talk to your child about feelings. Remind them that when they feel safe, they have a good feeling inside, and when they feel unsafe, they have a "yucky" feeling. Tell them that good feelings come when they make good choices and take healthy risks.

Bad feelings come when they make bad choices and take unhealthy risks that could hurt them or someone else. Tell your child if someone, even if they know them, makes them feel unsafe, remember to tell you or someone else they can trust. Explain to them that if someone asks them to do something, that it's okay to say no if they don't feel safe.

Tips for personal safety

- Help your child identify a list of their trusted people, people they can talk to if they feel unsafe, anxious, or even a little upset.
- Use every opportunity during everyday activities to talk to your child about themselves, how they are feeling, and the things that make them feel happy and safe.
- Remind them that you and their trusted people are there for them to talk to anytime they are feeling unsafe, a little worried, or unsettled no matter how small the concern is.

SAFE

PERSONAL SAFETY TIPS

Teach your child that when you are out and about or even at home, you may come in contact with a stranger, a person you don't know. Explain that most strangers are good people, but occasionally there is a bad person. It is really hard to tell which strangers have good behaviours and which strangers have bad behaviours. Teach your child that sometimes strangers can pretend to be friendly, offering them toys and lollies, or may be asking for their help. If they happen to come across a stranger that does this, they should just say "no thanks" and go straight to you (Mum or Dad) or another trusted adult.

Another great idea is to decide on a secret "safe word". A secret safe word is a word you create with your child that they don't share with anyone that they don't know or doesn't know the safe word. If someone asked them to come with them because they have said Mum or Dad asked them to collect them, they could say, "What is our 'safe word'?" and if they don't know it, they would know that person is not telling the truth.

Safety tip sayings

Say "No, I won't go" to strangers that want you to go with them.

Say "No, I can't help" to strangers that want your help.

Say "No thanks" to strangers that offer lollies and gifts.

SAFE

THE SUPER eSAFE KID

Just like in real life, online activities can never be risk free. Everything in life has risks, so when making a decision about your child's safety, you have to find a good balance so they can still be free to explore and enjoy their childhood.

The digital world has transformed how our children spend their childhood. It is continually evolving and changing as more children go online. The internet will bring out the best and the worst in human nature. It is up to parents and educators to show children how to navigate the internet safely to reduce threats and risks and develop the endless play and educational opportunities the digital world makes possible. As well as them learning and having fun, the internet helps your child to prepare for challenges in their childhood and can bring out their potential.

Like most things in life, we need a good balance of digital and real-life experiences. Too much digital time restricts opportunity to get out and explore the real world, and too little time limits the capacity of the digital world to enhance and shape their real-life experiences. The digital world offers greater access to learning and more social contact, especially for children living with physical, intellectual, financial, or remote location challenges. At times when we are required to practise social distancing, staying within our homes, or home-schooling, children can have online adventures and practise staying safe, just like in the real world. Safe and responsible use of technology is often referred to as "e-safety". E-safety is about being safe, kind, and making good choices online.

Get your child to imagine the digital world as a playground and a place to learn.

All the things we do in real life to stay safe, we need to do in the digital world, too. We have to "think safe and play safe".

HOUSE RULES FRAMEWORK

There are many ways for your child to explore the digital world via the internet, net for short, using either a phone, tablet, computer, or a smart TV. Before allowing them to use or watch these forms of technology, it is a good idea to decide on the "house rules".

Time
Decide for how long your child can spend on the net each day.

Values
Include family values just like you do in real life. For example, online be kind/respect others/think with your heart.

Safety Net
Ensure your search engines have child-safe zones, and put them in place. Teach them e-safety messages.

SAFE

MESSAGES FOR eSAFE KIDS

Ask Mum or Dad
– Get the OK to use the phone, tablet, computer, or smart TV.

Stop See Safe message
– Stop to See if it is Safe to do.

Be kind. Respect others and think with your heart.

Get Mum or Dad if you see or hear anything that gives you a yucky feeling.

Make good choices.

Get Mum or Dad if it rings or a pop-up comes online.

Choose a "safe word", a secret safe word, that you create with Mum and Dad, and don't share with anyone online or in real life that you don't know or who doesn't know the safe word.

MY TEAM

Explain to your child that sometimes you just can't do it on your own and you need the special people in your world to help you when you need help. Decide with your child the five people that they would like to take their hand. On a piece of paper, trace their hand. Get them to give you the five names and write them in each finger.

Who will take your hand?

- Teacher
- Grandparent
- Mum/Dad
- Friend
- Brother/sister
- Helper

Don't be afraid to ask for help. If the first person can't help you, go to the next.

FAMILY VALUES

Finding that common-sense approach that doesn't prohibit your child from activities and experiences that are important for their development will very much be based on your family practices, values, experiences, the environment you live in, and the capabilities of your child.

Your family's "live-by-practices"

Your family's "live-by-practices" are basically the family values and principles that you would like your family to live by and have them included in all aspects of daily life. To start, you might like to create a simpler name and include your child in deciding on the name. Also, engage your child in designing your practices.

Things to include may be:

How we communicate and act

- Make eye contact to demonstrate the full attention we are paying and are listening to the person.
- Acknowledge that you are being spoken to by giving a response.
- Practise a no-secrets policy unless it is a for a good reason like a surprise gift.
- Show gratitude.
- Respect others.
- Display manners and use "thank you" and "please" in everyday language.
- Be friendly and polite.
- Eat dinner together on as many nights as possible.
- Use meal-times as family chat occasions.
- Ban watching TV or using digital devices during meals.
- Ensure everybody gets to have one-on-one time regularly.
- Think with your heart.
- Be non-judgemental because everyone has a story.
- Accept others just the way they are.

Be a good role model who demonstrates family values

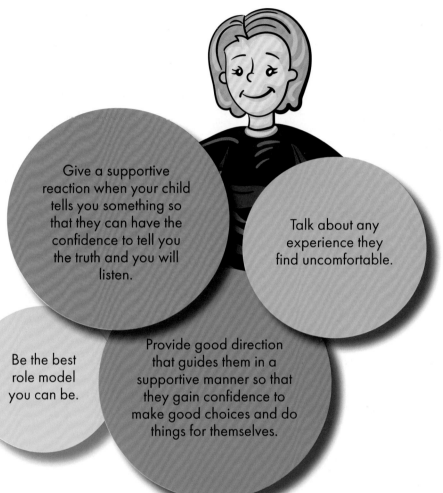

Give a supportive reaction when your child tells you something so that they can have the confidence to tell you the truth and you will listen.

Talk about any experience they find uncomfortable.

Be the best role model you can be.

Provide good direction that guides them in a supportive manner so that they gain confidence to make good choices and do things for themselves.

Recent Young Australian of the Year, Ash Barty, responded to her acceptance of the award by reflecting on family values:

I'm just trying to be true to myself and stick to the values that my mum and dad taught me, that my family have kind of instilled in me growing up.

SAFE

PLAY

Children learn best through play. Play is a fun thing. I can remember one of my favourite play activities was building pine-needle houses during playtime at kinder and school. We would form the pine needles into walls, make rooms, and sweep the dirt in between to form a perfect house and then role play in it for hours. Play is really important and should be the main activity for your child at this stage of their development. It is also a great way for you to engage fully and have heaps of fun with your child. Quite often the busyness takes time away from you and your child to play despite all the benefits that can be reaped from creating and exploring together through play. Play is the one activity children learn best from.

Don't be in too much of a hurry to encourage your child into adult roles; there is plenty of time for that in the coming years. All the things talked about in the risk-taking section can be gained through play if your child has lots of opportunities to do so like:

Gaining confidence

Understanding their capabilities

Knowing their limits

Building their resilience

Claiming their independence

Gaining emotional satisfaction

Making decisions

Developing social skills, like working in groups, sharing, negotiating with others, and resolving conflicts

Increasing their physical activity

Discovering their interests

SAFE

LEARNING FROM PLAY

Sometimes it is good to just step back and watch your child. You can learn a lot about their capabilities and their decision-making. By watching them, you can also get to know how creative they are, their interests, how they interact socially, and how they problem-solve and collaborate. Through play experiences, your child will learn to take risks that should involve some degree of challenge, creativity, and stimulation for developing their vital life skills.

Bowie, Frankie and Lewi playing at Messy Patch Torquay

SUPERVISION

When you are engaging in play with your child, something may come up where you need to provide some guidance. That's okay, but do it in a way that allows them to understand your reasoning, which may even include rules. Not all rules are bad. Play is actually not free of rules. Even in play, rules are important because they provide a framework for behaviours. However, when there are too many rules, over-regulation occurs, which restricts the way children play and the activities considered important for their development.

GOOD SUPERVISION

Good supervision doesn't mean "just watching". There are lots of supervision ideas. Sometimes it might mean just watching if they are engaging in uninterrupted play. But for your child to make good safe decisions, they need some GOOD SUPERVISION. By good supervision, we mean providing them with knowledge and experiences that helps them to become responsible risk-takers.

Yes, independent play is important, and so is good supervision, as it builds resilience and develops a sense of place, a sense of self-worth, social connectedness, and environmental knowledge. It might be as simple as taking a walk to the local shop to buy something, talking to elderly neighbours, or even sitting under a tree and watching the world around them. Giving them the freedom and privacy to make decisions about their own safety within their local environment is important. This will help them develop important "know-hows" that they will draw on throughout their lives. As environments become more complex, these know-hows will play a key role in supporting your child to become streetwise and a good risk assessor.

As I mentioned earlier, your child needs to be exposed to managed risks in order to learn from those experiences you give them. When your child manages situations and challenges safely, you as a parent will become confident that your child is capable of dealing with a particular situation. You, therefore, will have given your child a new level of trust because you feel confident that your child is more responsible, which leads to giving them more independence. Confidence is discussed more thoroughly in the first section. It is all about believing in yourself and your ability to do things and achieve.

SAFETY ZONE

Often another worry is that "my child is too friendly". It's also important not to be overcome by the advice that alerts to the dangers of children being too trusting. Being friendly and polite are actually qualities of good character we aspire our children to have. Children that become too suspicious and frightened can also experience dangers associated with these behaviours.

The safety zone

Establish your family's "safety zones" and design them together.

Places
- Home
- Grandparents' place
- Kinder/preschool

People
- Mum
- Dad
- Teacher

Practices
- Always tell your parents where you are going.
- Only go with people you can trust unless your parents have okayed it.
- Say no to things that give you an UNSAFE/YUCKY feeling.

SAFE

The best life and safety education you can give your child is to empower them to build a strong sense of identity and wellbeing. Love them, teach them to take responsibility for their emotions, and let them take managed risks like climbing monkey bars, riding bikes, and exploring our beautiful outdoors. It is hoped that you have gained some useful tips on how to help your child have a happy, healthy, and safe life with the attitude of letting kids be kids.

END NOTES

This book has been motivated by some inspirational people who have helped to shape the ideas behind Let Kids, Be Kids — Raising Happy, Healthy, and Safe Children.

WANT TO KNOW MORE

Initially my work was centred around children at the middle to upper primary level. At the time, this was when it was thought that children acquired the level of knowledge they needed to understand and begin to take control of their own behaviour and safety. It was while studying at Monash University, well into my PhD, that I realised this was far from the truth. One of the aims of the doctoral study was to find out when a child has the ability to manage behaviour and decisions about their own safety. The research project commenced at the primary school level but soon worked its way down to the early childhood stage, thanks to the support and guidance of two professors and an associate professor who were involved as supervisors. Professor Marilyn Fleer and Dr Joseph Agbenyega were from Monash University's Faculty of Education, and Professor Joan Ozanne-Smith from the Head Injury Prevention Research Unit at Monash University's Department of Forensic Medicine. It was a privilege and challenge to have a balance of educational and scientific thinkers in the mix of the study.

Marilyn based her child development theories on a "cultural-historical approach". This sounds awfully academic, but basically it means that culture and social interaction matters in human development. Her wealth of respected knowledge in the field has been built on the work of Vygotsky and the emphasis he placed on self-regulation and the ability to act with understanding. Influenced by his theories, other modern philosophers followed, who found that by the end of kindergarten, children should have the capability to act in a deliberate and planned manner in governing their own behaviour. So, this is the reason why the book has been devoted to the kindergarten/ preschool child. Although most kindergarten/preschool children are aged four or five the year before going into formal schooling, I try not to talk too much about age because a child's capabilities are based on far more than just age, which is another whole chapter for another time. However, our belief is that this is an opportune time to introduce valuable life lessons and positive personality empowerment time when children gain the ability to manage their own actions and take control of their emotions, a time when children become more independent, wanting to explore and ask questions about the things around them.

This is also a time for you to shine as a supporter and when your parenting skills have a favourable impact on your child's development and where reasoning plays a major role in the choices they make. Introducing injury prevention learning to your child is far more complex than teaching safety lessons as we have discussed. We need to consider much more: their personalities, the experiences you give them, and the human qualities we wish them to inherit to enable them to respond to situations and make good choices that result in positive outcomes. These are the foundation years for the little person in your life to become happy, healthy, and safe.

The work of Michael Adamedes, a clinical psychotherapist, has also influenced the thinking behind this book. He has built his philosophy on personality and the power of the unconscious mind that involves a diverse range of beliefs and cultures. Michael's way of thinking has helped shape my beliefs regarding the connection between human behaviour, personality, and the mindset when making better life choices that result in better self-awareness in children.

His book *Hello to Happiness* provides valuable knowledge and is well worth reading. If you would like to find out more about Michael's work, you can go to his website michaeladamedes.com.

Michael connects personality with determining the way we unconsciously respond to a situation, how we generate emotions, and the circumstances of our lives. Michael describes personality as a collective of a person's beliefs, emotions, and behaviour. According to Michael:

Your personality includes the conscious and unconscious memories in your mind and body. It is the result of all your experiences from conception onwards, plus the ancestral and genetic qualities you have inherited from your parents, grandparents, and forebears. Your personality determines your unconscious, habitual ways of responding to situations. However, your habitual responses are often attempts to protect yourself from rejection, scarcity, or danger and tend to create the opposite effect of what you intended, thus making you more unhappy (Adamedes, 2012, p. 19). His book *Hello to Happiness* is well worth reading.

Michael believes that 90 percent of our personality is inherited, made up of acquired positive and powerful traits handed down through the generations. So, you have created this little person in your life and they are who they are because of you, your parents, grandparents, and their genetic traits that make up their personality. The good news is that those things that you have inherited and that you don't love, in most cases, can be changed. Michael believes that when you accept responsibility for events in your life, you have a chance to change them so that they are more favourable and there is a positive path shift. There is also "epigenetics", which is more complicated and involves switching genes on and off. To understand what epigenetic means, you will need a crash course in biochemistry and genetics before learning exactly what it is. It's worth a Google, though. According to Michael, there are three variables that determine the quality of our lives: genetics, environment, and the ability to be in touch with our emotional and mental processes. When this occurs, he believes a person can rise above the perceived limitations that stem from genetic and environmental influences.

Another extremely knowledgeable person on health and happiness is Tyler Tolman who has built his philosophies and studies on cultures of the longest living humans. While some of his beliefs are quite controversial, he has spent much time on researching history and has established his practices and guidelines for a happy and healthy life on seven principles of health: air, water, wholefoods, sunshine, exercise, passion, and relationships.

In sections, this book has touched on assessing and managing risk, which is very much a subjective matter that is beyond the scope of this book. However, consideration needs to be given to various aspects of risk. First, there are certain types of risk that help children manage those risks — for example, safety education initiatives that we talk about in the book that teach children to swim or ride a bike. Second, there are also children who are risk-takers who may expose themselves to greater levels of risk. These children probably need more "good supervision" opportunities. Third, children are exposed to other benefits as a side effect of having activities to engage in that have a degree of risk. For example, the level of risk associated with outdoor play in consideration with the health and physical development benefits. The final consideration in supporting the need to engage in a level of managed risk-taking are the benefits, like building character and personality, that enables them to tackle challenges they face in their everyday lives.

Let Kids

Be Kids

Let Kids

Be Kids

THANK YOU

Thank you to all those people who has contributed to making this book a reality.

To Dr Richard Harris (Harry), Professor Marilyn Fleer, Michael Adamedes, Turia Pitt, Brittney Tasker-Gilbert and Matt Thiele for your stories and inspiration. Thanks George for featuring on the front cover of this book.

To the book design team – Teneille O'Connor for your artistic touch in co-creating the look and feel of the book. Your loyalty, having worked alongside me since 2005, is deeply appreciated. Also, to Dean Tonkin for your illustrations. They have brought the characters and my work to life. To Paul Beseler and Verve Portraits for producing most of the photos. Thank you also to Brenton Thomas, from Fresh Eyes Australia, for providing the editing assistance.

And a shout-out to the extraordinary team I work with at the KIDS Foundation – Janine, Carlee, Erynne, Nick, Beau, Teneille and Melissa – and the KIDS Board – Jo, Matt, Rimas, Margie, Hamish, Charles, Athol and Ian – who all share my passion for making a difference to the lives of young children.

Finally, a big thank you to my beautiful family. To my husband, Brett, and our children – Matt, Emma, Ben and Kate – who give my life purpose. Also to their partners – Melita, Adam, Whittney and Ricky – and to our beautiful grandchildren – Bailey, Chase, Nellie, Lewi, Frankie, Bowie, Alfie and Bella – and all the other little ones on the way.

To the millions of children, you have a voice and can speak and do for yourself; create a life of happiness, good health and find your safe places to be.

X O'Neill